GOOGLE CLASSROOM

The Ultimate Beginner's Guide

Table of Contents

Chapter 1..4

The Basics of Google Classroom..............................4

Simply Stunning..5

Classroom Features..6

Getting Started with Classroom

Other Important Reminders..10

Chapter 2..12

What Teachers can do with Google Classroom?.............12

Organization..12

Multitasking..13

Work with ease

Make use of online resources..15

Grading Process..15

Communication..16

Host Activities..18

Chapter 3..20

The Essence of Google Classroom to Educators..............20

Sharing Materials and Content Online....................21

Flipped Classroom..21

Productivity..22

Collaboration...22

More Functions for Teachers...................................23

Chapter 4..26

What Learners can do in Google Classroom?..............26

More Functions of Google Classroom for Students.28

Google Apps for Education...........................29

Student Perspective

Chapter 5..31

Google Classroom for Professional Development.....31

How Google Classroom Help...........................32

Google Classroom for Principals....................33

The Convenience of Being in One Classroom

Chapter 6..36

New Features and Uses of Google Classroom........36

Opportunities for Librarians............................39

Conclusion..41

Chapter 1

The Basics of Google Classroom

Learning Management Systems (LMS) are efficient applications that make electronic education possible and effective. One of the most powerful tools in this field is the Google Classroom. It offers a wide array of solution and expertise not only for students, teachers but also professionals. This tool makes teaching and learning more interactive and easy.

However, the Classroom is actually not a type of LMS as the classroom is more of a file management system. It aims to simplify the distribution and teaching process. Google Classroom works with other Google Apps used for education. This internet-based platform seamlessly functions with other features such as Gmail, Google Calendar and Google Docs. Because it is internet-based, it is cost-efficient and saves in the usual tangible materials used for teaching such as paper.

The platform makes life easier for its users specifically in classroom functions such as class assignment distribution, organization and communication. Using the Classroom, teachers and students can easily manage their everyday classroom activities. While there are various workflow solutions within Google Apps that educators are already using, it is undeniable that Classroom provides practical options. It has an instinctive interface with the right integration of tools.

To date, almost 10 million students and educators worldwide are actively using the platform, enjoying all the perks it offers. It has become their central place for learning, sharing knowledge, working together and exchanging ideas.

However, Google Classroom restricts the participation of the domain. Students and teachers should have a Google account which is specific to their school's domain. This will protect their information and privacy and other Google accounts.

Simply Stunning

Incorporating technology in every student and educators' daily lives will be certainly greeted with enthusiasm. Google Classroom is another tech-oriented approach to learning that is highly beneficial for teachers and students.

What most users look for in a software application or platform is that it has to be simple and user-friendly. It is not boring as it follows the latest in design trends, but keeping the design simple yet, elegant. Moreover, the app is absolutely free so almost everyone can utilize and gain benefits from it.

It makes the paperless classroom environment possible, allowing teachers to instantly gain access to their student's work. It also allows educators to manage multiple classes, create and distribute tasks, check and revised assignments and paperwork and handle other aspects of a digital classroom.

While security issues are very critical in cloud-based technology, one can be sure that the Classroom is safe since it is managed by Google. Many of its users describe Google Classroom as a life-saver that works hand-in-hand with educators. This tool helps them to save resources, keep their class organized, initiate participation and enhance the communication among their students. Indeed, it is one-stop shop that offers essential training, apps, products and resources for all its users.

Google Apps for Education is composed of 60+ applications including Calendar, Gmail, Doc, Sheets, Drive, Slides and Drawing.

Classroom Features

- Google Drive Integration – a Classroom folder will be automatically created in the teacher's Google Drive account. For every new class her or she creates, a sub-folder will be also created. However, the recent update disabled the download and printing the content. The teacher can also set admin alerts, and manage the sharing setting of their folders.

  The update is built to protect the contents of the classroom folders and helps teachers to control the sharing of the content within the Google Classroom.

- Class code and theme- similar with traditional classrooms, a class code will be generated for every class.

You can choose from a wide array of color themes and photos when creating classes. It also has the "About" page where you can provide information and essential links about the class.

- Communication- the teacher can send class announcements and assignments. They can also post questions about the subject matter and have the students discussed over it. Teachers and students can also comment on each other's assignments. Now they are also allowed to stick posts and move a specific post to the top.

- Organization- students in the Google Classroom will also have their own Classroom folder once they joined a class. Assignments in Google Docs will be automatically distributed to each student in the class.

- Google Forms- these are another useful tool in creating tests, quizzes and survey forms. Teachers can attach Google Forms to assignments and posts.

- Due dates- teachers are able to indicate due dates in their given assignments. One can also create assignments without due dates.

- Turn in and Return- once the student submitted their assignments on or before the due date, it will limit his access to a "Viewing Status". The teacher can start giving feedback or grading. If there are revisions to make, the status will be changed to "Editing Status" so the student can start working on it again.

- YouTube integration – teachers have the abilities to restrict and managed networks and YouTube videos that are considered acceptable in the classroom.

- Picture view- the entire class can see all their classes which give them an overview of the upcoming assignments for all their classes.

- Cloud technology- one of the most essential feature of Goggle Classroom is that it weaves together other education focused apps on Google such as Google Docs, Gmail, Sheets and Drive. This also eliminates time consuming tasks of accessing various resources and tools.

Google Classroom is no being used worldwide by schools with a GAFe or Google Apps for Education domain. It empowers not only the educators, but the students as well by creating a solid place to easily assign tasks and functions similarly to traditional classrooms.

Google Classroom will be also having its education-focused software on iOS and Android devices. We will expect teachers to carry their "class" at the palm of their hands. A paperless classroom, with very minimal resources, but is more functional. Students and educators alike can do a lot of things within the Classroom. The platform allows its users to be organized and manage multitasking effectively.

Getting Started with Classroom

Before you get started with Google Classroom, here are some important reminders.

- Users can come from various GAFe domains. The IT or administrator can white list the needed domains.

- Apparently, the application seamlessly works with Google browser. Although you can use other browsers, not all the features will run smoothly.

- Only the teacher can see ALL the comments being posted even they deleted it.

- It has a limit of 1000 students and 100 teachers.

- When using the classroom for the first time as a teacher, select the "Teacher" option. If not, your administrator will have to reset your account in the Google Apps control panel to change your role.

- Everyone must be using the same email domain since they will not be able to join if they use a different domain.

When you log-in for the first time, make sure to use the appropriate role of teacher or student. The assigned teacher can start creating the class by clicking the + button found in the upper right hand corner of the screen.

When a box pops up, you can add the class name and section. Then, set the details of the class in the "About" tab. You can put the class title, class description, room location and other random details. You can also add an administrator or a collaborating teacher so they can gain access to the classroom.

Teachers can also add resources and other needed materials such as a syllabus, classroom rules etc. Select the theme of the class or add a photo in the top section. Again, once you created the class, a Google Drive folder will be automatically created as well. It bears the same title as the name of the class. Assignments and announcements posted will be automatically added to the folder.

Next, the teacher can add or invite students by using the invite button where they can enter the student's email address or by giving them codes. The students can enter the class using the code by clicking the + button found on the main page.

The teacher can now set commenting rules. Click on the button that says "Students can post and comment" and choose from these settings.

- No restriction. Basically they can post and comment like what they usually do in Facebook.
- Students can only comment on the teacher's post.
- Or only the teacher can post and comment and students are not allowed.

Other Important Reminders

Remember that the teacher sees all the comments and posts of every student. Likewise, the teacher has three options for these comments; move to top, delete or mute. The move to top option will bring the post on top of the stream page. The "Delete" will completely erase the comment while the "Mute" option will remove a student's ability to post or comment in all posts.

The stream tab works like Facebook that whenever the teacher posts, it will be on top of the stream. This is also where all the other comments from the students show up. Users can have real-time view on the upcoming due dates.

One of the most favourite features of Google Classroom is that it allows teachers to monitor their students during their whole working process. Once the student opens the link to their assignment, the teacher can have a quick check on it.

Likewise, the folders that were automatically created once a classroom was created are mainly used for distributing and copying student files. Remember that these folders are not for outside use. If a teacher manually puts a file or a material in the classroom folder, the contents will not be visible to the students and will not be displayed.

Chapter 2

What Teachers can do with Google Classroom?

We believe that teachers are one of the most creative and innovative people in the world, hence, they are able to utilize the many functions of Google Classroom in various ways. Below are some of the functions of the Classroom to educators.

Organization

Organizing and managing a class is quite challenging, especially if you are holding multiple classes. The scheduling feature of the classroom is a unique way to create assignments with due dates. The deadline is clear for everyone in the class.

- All the students work will be put in a specific folder that is accessible from the teacher's Google Drive. The teacher can guide the students and give them feedback through the process of the task.
- Collecting their homework is also easy as these are submitted online. The teacher can provide feedback, even while the student is still working on assignment.
- Teachers will spend less time doing administrative tasks and paperwork. One can immediately ask a teacher if there is something that is not clear to him and the teacher can immediately respond.
- Teachers can also choose whether a certain document can only be viewed or edited.

- Every time the teacher posts an announcement, a question or an assignment, the Classroom will automatically send it to all the students. They will receive an email notification.
- If you want to send an email to a certain student, you can select his or her email address and simply compose and send an email.

Multitasking

The Classroom helps teachers to cut down their workload. They can do even more than just spending their time photocopying exams and disseminating it to students on the day of the examination. This is also an advantage for students since they no longer need to write down notes and copy everything that should be written on the board.

- Google Classroom is also suitable for co-teaching. One can invite another teacher to his or her class to do team-teach. Just open the course and click the "About" option to invite a teacher by just entering the teacher's email address.
- Teachers can do different tasks with Google Classroom. They can create and disseminate assignments and start class discussions. The Goole Drive also enables teachers to send their handouts online. Learners can also access the stream and get notified for an upcoming exam or be reminded of their assignment due dates.
- The original version of Classroom has no option for "save as draft" when posting an assignment. The teacher has to publish his or her work once he used the assignment option. The recent updates make the scheduling of assignments possible. The user only has to choose the scheduling option to select a specific time and date when the assignment is ready for posting.

Work with ease

Teachers also find Google Classroom as a simple yet, functional application for everyone. They can easily assess their students and gauge how much they learn. Because of the Classroom's mobile apps, they can stay connected and monitor the progress of the class even when they are attending other matters.

- Teachers within the same districts that were using different domains can still share files and content with each other. There is also a feature called Reuse posts that allows teachers to reuse announcements, assignments and questions that they believe are still applicable to their current class. You can copy the post as is or have modifications before posting it again.

- Google Classroom is easy to set-up and teachers can easily create a class, share knowledge and information, prepare and distribute assignments, post and answer questions and give announcements.

- The entire process and workflow is simple in paperless. Everyone in the class can work in a very timely and efficient in manner in just a single place. No need for various tools to pull-up.

- Google Classroom is also accessible to various devices which make it an ideal application for a Bring Your Own Device environment also called BYOD. Teachers can access the classroom through their smartphones, laptops, PC or phablets.

- Even teachers need relaxation and some "me time". They can plan their vacations ahead by scheduling assignments, questions for posting and announcements to be posted on a specific date and time. They will receive notifications via SMS and email once their schedule posts go live.

Make use of online resources

Apparently, students are into different social sites and they have an access to most online resources. Most of them have accounts on these sites. Using the Google Classroom, the teacher can easily give them assignments with a link for instructions such as a video tutorial. Others encourage their students to regularly submit a blog or journal entry.

- The assignments can be in a Google file such as presentation, spreadsheet and doc or can have a link of YouTube video and other materials. Multimedia projects can be submitted in different formats. For an instance, a documentary can be submitted with an attached script, a story board or a presentation.

- Because everything is done online, we are also able to save trees since there is no need for hard copies. Everything such as presentations, spreadsheets and documents can be distributed digitally. Online assignments can also have attachments and web links.

- Any kind of multimedia such as audio files, videos, documents, images and PDF can be also attached or store in the classroom's Google Drive. These various online resources will encourage the students to come up with their own materials.

Grading Process

The grading process is considered a tedious task for a teacher handles more than one student. Checking and grading examinations, quizzes, long essays and various assignments in different classes will take plenty of their time.

- Google Classroom makes it easier to do such task. A teacher can record all the grades in a spreadsheet and add feedback then return it to Classroom. Don't worry because students will not see their grades unless you press the "Return" button.
- They can also instantly monitor who among their students have completed their assignments and give them real-time feedback and grade them instantly.
- After the assignments are turned in, the teachers can see who among the students submitted or did not submit their work.
- Teachers can grade their students in different ways; they can choose from one of the numerical values provided in the system or have a customized value. They can also upload grades through CSV file. Students can see their grades on their accounts in Google Class.

Communication

Communication is important between teachers and students. Google Classroom can improve and strengthen the bond of teachers and students. They are able to talk to each other through comments and feedback on their assignments and be in the moment.

- Like a traditional classroom, the question and answer portion during or after every discussion is significant. This enhances the students' communication skills and making learning an interactive and fun activity for everyone.
- Teacher's can now use the Create a Question" feature to initiate a class discussion. It can also be done for survey or poll to gauge the class' understanding of the topic. There are two options to do this: you can have a short answer or a multiple choice type of question.
- The multiple choice type is suitable for a quick check on the students' understanding of the subject discussed such as math equations and

solutions or understanding of a literary piece. The short answer type of question allows students to engage in discussion through comments where they can reply to one another.

- By posting a topic or a question, the teacher can instantly start an online discussion. This initiates an online forum where learners can give and share their own insights among other online student. It is an efficient way to answer queries, solve problems and expand their knowledge.

- We know how eager the students are to leave school and forget all the assignments and school- related stuff during school breaks. However, teachers notice that their students would like to keep in touch and keep the class open while they are on breaks. It keeps them connected as a community.

- Teachers can offer positive feedback for everyone to see through Google Stream. It is an effective way to encourage students to exert more effort with their assignments and motivate others who are having difficulties dealing with their own works.

- Moreover, it gives voice to those shy-type students who never raise their hands in a traditional classroom setting.

- A physical school environment, actual recitations, discussion and presentations in front of the class could be dreadful for some students. In Google Classroom, they can find the stream less frightening, so introvert students can still show their creative side. It can also help teachers to motivate them to participate in online discussions. They can also come up with game-based topics to promote camaraderie, trust and teamwork among students.

Since it's launched, educators are using Google Classroom's streaming to host various activities, discussions and debates. It is a collaborative way to engage the class to have their own discussions by posting questions or giving answers. This can help the teachers to keep their students focused on their on-going lesson.

Reducing workload

Teachers tend to have too much workload every school year. For an instance, a teacher has to teach three courses, handle five to eight classes, work at least five days a week and create several exams, check attendance, grade students etc.

Plus, there should be allocated time for student counselling, come-up with presentation or attend school meetings. There are other academic activities that need their time as well. Google Classroom can help them lessen their workload and keep them organized.

This integration of Google Classroom in our modern day school should not be an option. This is something that is crucial to prepare students for the future. However, the biggest challenge for educators here is how to seamlessly manage and use digital tools. One should be familiarized with the equipment and software, knows how to integrate it with their lesson plan and adjusting their traditional approach to make it appropriate.

This is when Google Classroom will be highly appreciated. This platform offers various benefits and aids for teachers and students. Going digital and classroom technology integration is easier with the classroom.

Prior to the classroom, teachers are already figuring out how to simplify the complicated workflow of distributing and turning in students' homework. Google Classroom helps eliminate current issues in the physical classroom while giving educators the gift of time to attend to other important matters.

Chapter 3

The Essence of Google Classroom to Educators

More than just making the workloads easy, Google Classroom helps educators, teachers and facilitators to motivate their students. The possibilities are endless as how they can utilize the many features of Google Classroom for the betterment of the students.

Today's generation is more inclined into their devices and gadgets and almost everyone knows how the internet works. Thus, modern teachers find Google Classroom a logical solution to get the most out of the digital era. The application also aids them in adapting their lessons to online education.

The education process could be more productive when everything is well organized. The Classroom has fewer distractions compared to traditional classrooms, allowing students to exert more of their time and effort to learning the lessons.

And because modern children are avid users of technology, giving them school works and assignments online would be a better setting for them. Now you can get them involved in the educational process where they can enjoy and participate.

Creating lessons from scratch will require you plenty of time and resources. Moreover, as a teacher, one must keep in touch and closely monitor the class, check their assignments, give proper feedback, answer their questions and grade them simultaneously.

Fortunately with Google Classroom, you can "recycle" or modify your previous lessons and even share it to your students wherever they are. By just providing a link to these materials such as an uploaded book or attached images, everyone in the class can get access to it.

The Classroom also has a discussion thread where students can see previous posts, links and questions. This is great in saving time because they just have to re-read the threads related to their queries.

Flipped Classroom

Flipped classroom refers to a type of learning or an instructional strategy which reverses the physical or traditional learning environment by moving activities, resources and instructional content online.

Students have now access to learning materials, even they are outside the classroom, such as watching instructional videos and reading lectures or articles online. They can do this at home while class time will be allocated only for discussions, problem-solving, question and answer portion and debates.

Google Classroom is said to be an efficient tool to flip an entire class. You see, in a flipped classroom, learning could be personalized to cater every a student's learning pace and ability. It is as if giving them the ownership of their own learning process and development and Google Classroom helps them to achieve such.

The Classroom is a safe venue for discussions while students can review the contents and materials. Teachers on the other hand, can immediately clarify misconceptions or further explain the topics to students.

Productivity

Again, Google Classroom is a teacher on-stop shop when it comes to class activities. They are able to streamline the digital workflow, push out announcements, disseminate assignments and engage students to interact during class. Both students and teachers can gain benefit with the workflow.

They can use their own device and gain access to student's work anywhere as long as they have an internet connection.

Collaboration

To date, 30 million faculty, staff and students are using Google Apps for Education. The free suite for schools includes other educational platforms and tools from Google. The Chromebooks are being used by thousands of students and teachers and use Google apps for school-related matters.

In Classroom teachers are able to co-teach a class and students can interact with the teachers and other students. Everything becomes possible with Google Classroom and one can learn even outside the confines of four walls.

- They can align their curriculum with other educators given that they have the same domain.

- Share data and materials with professional learning community.

- Gather weekly or annual feedback from students through Google Forms.

- Share writing samples, anonymously in the classroom.

- Discuss assignment criteria and other requirements.

- Developed mobile learning experiences for students.

- Post announcements for parents.

- Come up with a list of the approved resources that the students can use.

- Divide the resources according to criteria such as student's level, difficulty of comprehension, groupings etc.

- Encourage interaction among students through commenting to each other's posts or assignment. Promote interaction among students, schools and faculties.

- Manage the setting for viewing, editing, copying and downloading of files to protect the classroom file.

- "Talk" to students through private messaging, especially to those who are hesitant or are shy to ask questions.

- Publish the common accessed resources and websites so everyone in the class will gain access to the same information, same links, and same materials.

- Promote the use of smart phones and other gadgets for formal learning. They can access their assignments, web links and files on a BYOD device. More than just being an entertaining device, they will consider their gadgets an important tool for learning.

- Teach students about annotated research papers with specific styles such as APA and MLA.

- Create digital versions of lessons, texts, questionnaires, materials, snapshots and PDFs and provide access to these folders.

- Share Google Slides presentation where students can work and edit. Enable them to add information and insert comments on other slides.

- Posting important notes in the announcement section to allow students to easily pull up these notes. This way, they can focus more on the discussion rather than taking down notes.

- Aside from learning the subject, teachers are also allowing students to explore the system and apply the things they learn in the classroom in actual scenarios.

- It helps them eliminate cheating during examinations since students are working on their own and teachers can easily monitor their activities within the classroom.

- Teachers can easily assess their students' studying habits and give them prompt feedback.

- Create student groupings based on their interests, skills levels, subject matter and other factors for learning.

Apparently, Google Classroom offers a myriad of benefits and functionalities that make teaching and learning more effective. It has become a powerhouse for both educators and learners. It helps them to survive especially the crucial parts of learning. It also facilitates collaboration which is an integral part of every student's success.

It also gives learners and educators a safe place for communication that helps them to build trust between them. Teachers also become well informed of their students' standing in class and aid them toward learning process. Lastly, most teachers admit they have poor handwriting. With online comment and feedback, students can clearly understand what their teachers have to say about their performance and assignments.

Chapter 4

What Learners can do in Google Classroom?

Educators in this digital age can take advantage of numerous technologies that aim to enhance their teaching process while assisting the students for fast learning. Google apps are considered the most readily available and user-friendly tools that teachers and students can use. Moreover, Google apps enhance the educational experience through better collaboration, organization and digital literacy.

In Google Classroom, the teacher is the administrator therefore, only he or she can see the entire class, but students can do various activities using the platform. Students also have limits and restrictions such as downloading and sharing the content of the class drive or inviting other students to your class.

However, Google Classroom still has a lot to offer for students. It encourages them to learn ideas from one another through their teacher's guidance. Here, they join in the process of learning which later helps them to build confidence.

SHARING

There is a Stream tab where you can share your thoughts or answer for the entire class to see. Students are also allowed to attach documents, files, web links and videos to their message. Likewise, the class can access materials and resources within the classroom that they can use with their assignments.

ASSIGNMENTS

Students no longer have an excuse of forgetting their assignments at home since their assignments are accessible in the Classroom including the due dates. Just lick the button "View All" to see all the assignments. It also has *To-Do* and *done* tabs that you can click to mark the status of each assignment.

They can even add a new document, file or link to the assignment box. To comment in an assignment, press the Add Comment area that can be found at the bottom part of the assignment box. Be reminded that your comments are in public and can be seen by everyone in the class.

KEEP TRACK

Another cool feature is that assignments will appear on the Google Calendar. It is a substantial way for students to monitor and keep track of their assignments at a glance. They are allowed to change the color since every class is color coded. They can also set the calendar to notify them though SMS pop up or email reminders ahead of their due dates.

Students can also see their progress of their assignments. Because Google Classroom support the BYOD method, the whole learning process is convenient for both teachers and students.

FEEDBACK

Another great thing with Google Classroom is that it entitles students to comment back on the teachers note to his or her assignment. It provides them a more dynamic experience since traditional classrooms are not usually like this. Students will submit their assignments and the teachers will check and return it without discussing important pointers.

More Functions of Google Classroom for Students

Aside from the functions mentioned above, we still have a long list of the benefits and functions of the Classroom.

- Add a feedback to a specific lesson that is not clear to you and save it to a different folder so you can revise it.
- Ask questions privately to your teacher.
- Create digital portfolios of your favourite work for future reference.
- Create and monitor their own growth using Google Sheets.
- Email other students as a group or individually and initiate conversation.
- Submit assignments with attachments such as voice clips, drive files, videos and links.
- Reduce and even eliminate the use of paper and spend time copying and distributing the work.
- Get accountable with homework due dates as it appears in their Google Calendar.
- Students can now participate in "read alouds" by replying to questions. They are able to engage in accountable talk without fear of "talking" and explaining themselves.
- The app is flexible, accessible and easy to manage by both learners and instructors. Students can explore through various online instructional materials.
- Although Google Classroom is only accessible for students in an educational institution, anyone can access other Google apps such as slides, docs, presentation and spreadsheet.
- Google Classroom is mobile-friendly so there should be no issues using it on mobile devices.
- The classroom promotes collaborative work among students and instructors through feedback and comment features.

Google Classroom not only helps educators, but students as well, in terms of workflow and organization. Its powerful features make it an efficient tool to aid students in various aspects of learning such as communication, multitasking and productivity.

Moreover, we know for a fact that assignments can take most of the time of the students but, with Google Classroom the assignment process is a lot easier. By just clicking a button, they were able to access their assignment and work on it even when they are not at home or on-the-go. No need for notebooks, pens and heavy books to bring with them since all the necessary materials are accessible in their Classroom.

Another great thing about Google Classroom is that automatically titles the assignments and documents from the students. Anything that the teacher creates for the students will be automatically shared within the classroom. The teachers can easily monitor the progress of their students and give comments, making students more accountable.

Google Apps for Education

Aside from Google Classroom, students can get advantage of other educational tools from Google called Google Apps for Education. Basically, this is a free suite of services that contain apps such as Google Calendar, Gmail, Presentation, Google Docs and Spreadsheets which are all necessary for learning. These apps and even the storage are free!

Moreover, students and teacher's privacy are both secured and cannot be used without their permission. There are also no Google Ads when they use Google Search. To make the experience more worthwhile, Chromebooks are being used in schools.

These are web-based computers that help users to easily manage the Classroom and other Google Apps. Chromebooks are available in different devices.

Student Perspective

According to surveys and online polls, students mostly agree that Google Classroom is helpful too. Everything can be done easily, from joining the class to submitting their assignments. Because of the classroom's unlimited storage, their files and materials online are safe plus, they can add their own materials too.

However, other students would feel intimidated and afraid especially those who are from rural areas where the access to internet connection is limited. They tend to feel pressured when they are instructed to use Google Classroom. In general, students feel the need for training to effectively use Google Classroom and to harness its various benefits.

They think of the classroom as an efficient learning tool. It allows them to upload videos such as recorded performances that they can watch repeatedly. Likewise, the classroom is helping them to enhance their presentation on any given topic.

Chapter 5

Google Classroom for Professional Development

Technology helps improve our daily activities by providing us easy alternatives. Likewise, it enables us to do more things and become productive. Google Classroom is no doubt one of the best platforms today. And while Google Classroom is primarily designed to cater to students and teachers in a usual classroom setting, users have found more creative ways on how they can utilize the application and take advantage of its features.

Now here comes professional development. This is a crucial part of developing and preparing students for real-life situations. Schools and districts can now use the Classroom to organize and come-up with professional development content for educators.

Professional development has been always a challenge for administrators and educators. Lack of professional development usually results to workplace stress. Hence, it is important that everyone in the school organization should work closely and to come up with effective professional development tools.

Google Classroom is not only for classroom teachers, but it is also now considered a methodical platform for learning professional development.

How Google Classroom Help

It is as similar when teachers spend days and even weeks to attend the usual seminar before and during the school year. With Google Classroom, teachers can easily create their presentations and training materials and send it to other participants.

Educators who are in the same classroom can share and make use of various resources such as multimedia files, links, eBooks, slides and other documents within the classroom. Like students and teacher, the participants can communicate real-time during the training.

Teachers can start from scratch in creating learning objectives, teaching strategies and tasks for students with the help of other teachers. It allows administrators and teachers to customize learning through interactive lessons.

- he principal, teacher or team leader will create a course and invite other educators to join the course. This will serve as their training session venue. He or she can create multiple courses according to what will be taught to the class. For schools that have various departments, the Team Lead can create a course for every subject.

- hen, the Team Lead will now choose if he or she will post an announcement or to initiate discussion in the class. An agenda can be attached before the meeting and all the participants can modify it real-time.

- hey can upload instructional videos or co-create assessments and share it to the whole class. The trainer can also share PowerPoint slides and handouts to other participants via the Announcement and Assignment tabs.

-

    e or she can make individual copies and attached documents and send it to each participant so that they can also use it when teaching to their own class.

Google Classroom is a great place for educators to work and collaborate on their projects. They can access their materials in a specific folder in the classroom and reuse these materials in the future.

And just like the usual Google Classroom for students, the Team Lead can also post questions regarding the training and the teachers can answer and give feedback individually or by group. They can do this on-the-spot or in a given due date for the assignment.

In other trainings, the Team Lead requires the teacher to produce proof of knowledge to gauge how much they learn from the session and grade their assignments.

Google Classroom for Principals

Even principals and school administrators can take advantage of the benefits of Google Classroom. They can utilize it to lead and share instruction, to guide their faculty and provide them with important information.

The principal can create a class to disseminate new forms, guidelines, examination pointers and other materials. The teachers in the classroom will automatically receive an email whenever the principal adds a new item.

All the educators in the course are considered students, hence, they can communicate with each other. They can initiate support, share ideas etc. They can also conduct planning sessions in real time and collaboratively develop common assessments.

The Classroom allows them to mix modern skills in teaching with the best practices that teachers are using for centuries. They are able to integrate technology with creativity. Students have more options as how they are going to explore, create and learn new things.

The Convenience of Being in One Classroom

- Almost every day, educators receive emails such as announcements, memorandum, documents and other files with numerous attachments. These can quickly fill their inboxes and might cause them to overlook which among the email is important. Google Classroom enables teachers to sort this efficiently.

- This is an effective and safe place to share regular and even high risk information. The messages are also easy to find and can be accessed anytime they want.

- It is easier to streamline information among staff and educators and have a centralize information. All the files can be found in one place.

- The Classroom is where a greater collaboration takes place while encouraging peer-to-peer learning system and promotes problem-based approach to learning.

- Educators can show support for each other by answering queries and sharing materials.

Google Classroom has indeed sparked a trend and introduced various tools from Google for Education suites. Teachers can now confidently use technology in teaching their students while also learning from other educators and in their online community.

Google Classroom users also believe that this increase the collaborative working. Compared to traditional devices and the physical classroom setting, education experts found various barriers to better learning. Old devices such as photocopiers, projectors and even computers will require annual maintenance and upgrade to cope up with the demands of school activities.

The school also has to pay for different software, applications, licenses and security that adds-up to the expenses. While using Chromebooks with educational tools from Google is way too cost-effective.

Chapter 6

New Features and Uses of Google

Classroom

Like any other platform, application or method, Google Classroom is also subject to some changes and upgrade. Apparently it has a lot to contribute to the Learning Management System industry and makes a paperless classroom possible. Currently, it is now being used by academic institutions, but it could also be used for corporate training in the future.

The recent updates of the platform have brought its users more functions and have given them more reasons to use Google Classroom.

- Quizlet Class- now, the teacher can easily create a quizlet upon creating the class. Once your Google Classroom account is up and running and you already have a Quizlet account, you can link it together. When you invite students to join your class, Quizlet will notify them via email.

- Uploading of playing tests – in a music class, students regularly uploads or record playing tests as part of their requirements. Once uploaded, the teacher and students can view it and leave feedback. They can also be graded instantly which, speeds-up the whole process. Plus, students were able to listen again to their playing test and figure out how to improve.

- Out-of-class viewing party- these days, teachers also incorporate important events, live performances, speeches, debates, movies and TV shows in teaching their classes. With Google Classroom, it is easier for teachers to engage their students by adding posts or questions that are noteworthy to the subject.

- Exit tickets or warm-up questions- teachers can conduct a quick assessment before or after the class by allowing students to participate in question-driven discussions. They can answer your posted questions and you also have the ability to restrict their ability to view each other's answers.

- Flubaroo is a Google Sheet add-on that can be used for long examination that is either true or false matching questions or a multiple choice one. Let Flubaroo grade the text and it will provide you a detailed result of the grading results.

- Multiple classes' discussion- Google Classroom is not only for your classmate, but for your schoolmates as well. With its new co-teacher feature, teachers can share a class in the Classroom. This means more classes can participate and interact in a certain discussion which will result to better collaboration.

- Photo for assignment- almost every tablet and smartphones come with cameras so everyone can easily take a quick snap. Now students can make a discussion or ask a question and even create an assignment based on relevant pictures.

- Forums- an entire grade level can now interact and share knowledge with each other through a forum. There could be multiple administrators and teachers assigned as moderators. You can also do it for the entire school to serve as a private hub for students and teachers.

- Poll question- this is highly useful for math teachers. They can turn real-world math problems into poll questions so students can determine the answer by using their math skills. Still, they need to have an explanation and show their solution on how they came to their answer. Poll questions are also ideal to gather feedback.

- Guided reading- the question feature of Google Classroom is a great way to post questions for testing student's vocabulary. Divide them in various guided reading group and come up with the list of words that they will study.
- Post a link- linking digital resources and educational videos to posted questions can increase the students' ownership. Teachers are also able to promote flipped classroom.
- In a recent update, Google acknowledges the importance of guardians and parents to a student's success thus, they would like to keep them updated. School leaders and teachers can now give real-time feedback to parents and guardians. However, this feature will be available later this year wherein parents will get notifications via email. They need to sign-up so they can receive weekly updates and email digests to help them monitor their student's progress at school upcoming assignments and other important announcements.

  This feature will engage parents and guardians to motivate and keep track of their students.

Modern era educators are familiar with free web-based platforms. It allows them to save resources and time while making it easier to create and distribute assignments. For Google Classroom users, they consider it a game changing platform that makes life easier and better.

However, like any technology integration, there should be limits and restrictions. Teachers should set the rules on what is appropriate and what is not in the classroom. Determine what is best for the students and what works fine with the class.

Opportunities for Librarians

Librarians and many other educational institutions are also making use of the technology by utilizing Google Slide, Google Forms, YouTube and Google Docs. They have adopted Google Education's platform to collaborate.

Google Classroom is the combination of Google's powerful tools. Aside from educators, librarians also believe that the Classroom will provide unique opportunities that will promote student's learning and participation. On the other hand, Google Classroom can support librarians by streamlining instruction for those who have credit-bearing classes.

When the classes are completed, the teachers can place it in the "Archive". Hence, future users will have continued access to the resources within that specific Classroom but they are not allowed to modify them. This creates a great opportunity for librarians.

- They do not have to be associated with a certain class. He or she can create a new class and add students.
- Unlike the regular classes, the class duration does not matter here. It can be a one-shot session or could be good for one semester. There is no specific time period to use Google Classroom. It can be used to provide open instructional workshops.
- Librarians can share the class code so students can join them. It offers a place to meet the students even before the actual meeting.
- Participants can share worksheets, surveys or preparatory content while discussing with one another.
- The classroom is an awesome place to bring in a large number of students especially, if the librarian has multiple sections in one course. Moreover, the librarian does not need to access personal profiles or folders of

students. He or she can be added as a librarian and provide instructions without students' grades and other confidential materials.

In general, students' overall experience in library instruction using Google Classroom is highly favourable. They are already familiar with the interface since they were already using Google tools. No more saving of files on a school computer because all of their files will be automatically saved in the classroom.

All these collaborative tools from Google have been adopted both the academic and the non-academic institutions. It allows librarians to expand their reach and influence. In general, Google Apps for Education offers numerous advantages but some of the most essential ones include the ability to access stuff online such as email, grades, assignments and other important documents. This eliminates the need to USB drives and hard drives. Most importantly, these features are free!

Conclusion

Most of us can recall those moments in our lives when we idly sit in a classroom, but we were not really focused and listening to our teachers. Such scene is still familiar in school settings these days. This traditional method of learning promoted teacher-centered classrooms and give lesser options for students.

We get used by instructors giving us information, students copying what is written on the board, teachers disseminating homework or test papers and the rest of reading and comprehension improvement will be left to the learners.

Although this traditional method could be effective for some students, many of them were forced to be just plain receivers of information instead of motivating them to engage and participate in the learning process.

With the help of technology and assimilation of various applications, a new learning model has developed. The digital era has penetrated our physical classrooms which removes the teacher-centered method of learning.

Learning has now become more collaborative and focuses more on student's progress in the classroom. Google Classroom indeed, is preparing students for the future. Apparently, we need to know how technology works and by training them young, they will be able to communicate and participate in their careers in the future. The Classroom is helping them to be familiarized and comfortable with the technology.

Google Classroom is also increasing student engagements and keeping them motivated by allowing teachers to motivate them in plenty of ways. Likewise, it gives them the latest information and trend. Web-based contents and materials are also accessible to them. Classrooms all around the world can soon be connected to each other that will broaden information.

For educators, Google Classroom makes it easier for them to deliver instructions while keeping their lesson student-centered. Now they have more time for discussions and answering questions or conducting problem-solving instead of doing and checking homework. Students also have adequate amount of time to understand the subjects.

Immediate assistance from the teacher is a must for students to continually grow and Google Classroom only enhances this aspect. Google Classroom and other learning applications will never replace our teachers, but these tools can help them improve every aspect of learning.

Made in the USA
Lexington, KY
13 September 2016